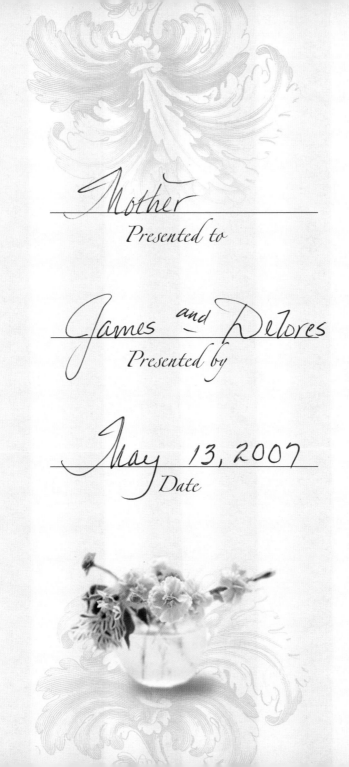

Mother
Presented to

James _{and} Delores
Presented by

May 13, 2007
Date

Dear Mom

*special thoughts to share
of hope, love, and appreciation*

Dear Mom
ISBN 1-40372-038-X

Published in 2006 by Spirit Press, an imprint of Dalmatian Press, LLC.
Copyright © 2006 Dalmatian Press, LLC. Franklin, Tennessee 37067.

Editor: Lila Empson
Writer: P. Barnhart
Text Designer: Whisner Design Group

06 07 08 09 WAI 10 9 8 7 6 5 4 3 2 1

14952

*Her children stand up
and call her blessed.*

Proverbs 31:28 NIrV

Contents

Introduction

Dear Mom, thank you for being who I need and knowing what I need. Your insight and timing are amazing. All my life you have been there exactly when I needed you. When I was little and got hurt, you appeared instantly with washcloth, ointment, and bandage. Anything that hurt, upset, or threatened me brought you quickly to my side. When I cried, the tears didn't get all the way down my face before you wiped them off. When I was sad, you smiled and laughed me into a better mood. When I was mad, you reasoned me back into a calmer disposition. You knew when I was disappointed about something. You understood those times I didn't feel adequate for what I was trying to do. Nothing about me escaped you.

What a great mother you were as I grew up. As I entered each phase of life, you entered it with me. You anticipated my new experiences and prepared me for them. You helped me meet the challenges of relating to other people. When I was tempted to compromise a value or principle, you encouraged me to stick to what is best. When I was too dependent on you, you affirmed my ability to do things for myself.

What a wonderful mother you are.

Thank you, Mom.

Mother Says So

Encourage each other and build each other up,
just as you are already doing.
1 Thessalonians 5:11 NLT

A ten-year-old boy was working in a factory in Naples before child labor laws were put in place. He worked long and hard because his mother was convinced he had a good singing voice and, by working in the factory, he could earn money for singing lessons.

He got together enough money to pay a teacher but, after a couple of lessons, his music teacher said he had little talent and it was a waste of money and time to continue. The boy's mother, a poor peasant woman, was not easily put off. She told her son he had the talent to become a good singer and encouraged him every way she could. They found another teacher, and the boy's mother went barefoot instead of buying shoes so she could save money for music lessons. Between her sacrifices and the boy's factory work, the music lessons continued.

The talent the boy's mother had seen blossomed and bore fruit that would never be forgotten. The boy would grow up and astonish audiences everywhere. He would sing before presidents and kings. Because of his mother's conviction and encouragement, Enrico Caruso became one of the greatest tenors the world has ever known.

Words of encouragement fan the sparks of ability into the flame of accomplishment. Abraham Lincoln's dying mother called her small son to her bedside and whispered, "Be somebody, Abe."

Dear God,
thank you for a mom
who makes me feel I can
do what I need to do.
With her on my side, I
am so much more.
Amen.

Always a Mother

I will teach you the way you should go;
I will instruct you and advise you.
Psalm 32:8 GNT

Carletta, in her early sixties, was expecting her four children and their nine offspring for a holiday dinner in two days. As always, she had a special little present for each of the grandchildren laid out in the game room downstairs. She had also checked the movie section of the paper and would take the grandchildren to see the latest film starring their favorite action hero.

Right now, Carletta was in the kitchen baking for the gang. Several requests had been made, and she was filling them one by one. But the request for a certain chocolate concoction had her stymied. She hadn't made it in years and couldn't find the recipe in any of her books. She looked through a couple of drawers where she informally filed an array of recipes, some scribbled on small scraps of paper, but nowhere could she find what she needed.

Then she remembered where she had first eaten that particular dessert delight. It had been at her mother's table more than fifty years before. It was a favorite her mom prepared for her dad at least once a week. Remembering that, she went to the phone and called the assisted-living complex where her eighty-seven-year-old mother had lived for almost five years. "Mom," she began the conversation, "I need your help on something."

Mom, your children will always need you. They will listen to what you say, learn what you know, follow where you lead, and desire your encouraging presence always.

Dear God,
thank you for a mom
who knows the answers
to my questions, some-
times before I ask them,
and understands what
I need at all times.
Amen.

Words of Hope & Encouragement

Fear not, for I am with you; be not dismayed,
for I am your God. I will strengthen you, yes,
I will help you, I will uphold you with
My righteous right hand.

Isaiah 41:10 NKJV

The LORD is the friend of those who obey
him and he affirms his covenant with them.

Psalm 25:14 GNT

Let us . . . . approach the throne of grace with
confidence, so that we may receive mercy and
find grace to help us in our time of need.

Hebrews 4:16 NIV

The LORD's lovingkindnesses indeed never cease,
for His compassions never fail. They are new every
morning; great is Your faithfulness.

Lamentations 3:22–23 NASB

Be at rest once more, O my soul,
for the LORD has been good to you.

Psalm 116:7 NIV

Thoughts to Share

The most important person on earth is a mother.
She has built something more magnificent than
any cathedral—a dwelling for an immortal soul.

Joseph Cardinal Mindszenty

I learned more about Christianity from my
mother than from all the theologians of England.

John Wesley

God created us to be in families. We have a
natural hunger to be a part of something that gives
us a sense of acceptance, affirmation, and being
needed and appreciated.

Stormie Omartian

You can fool all of the people some of the time
and you can fool some of the people all the time,
but you can't fool a mom.

Josie Hinkins

My mother was a simple, understanding,
loving, and courageous woman who gave me
both tools and weapons to help in living my life.

Jackie Robinson

You Promised

I will prove to you that I will keep my promise.
Isaiah 38:7 CEV

All his life, Eric has been glad his mom held him to his promise, and he has told her so many times. When Eric was in high school, he played basketball. Just before his senior year, his dad got transferred to another town. Nobody wanted Eric to miss his last year of basketball, and there was soon a plan to keep him in town for his senior year. He could live with neighbors down the street, and others would help him out.

Eric's parents agreed to the plan, on one condition. They'd let him stay if he'd go to the college they'd both graduated from. The school was academically renowned and had a strong religious program. Eric agreed, even though the college did not have an intercollegiate basketball team. Eric stayed in town his senior year, had a good season on the team, and was offered a basketball scholarship at another college. He accepted the offer and made plans to go. He told his parents over the phone and they came to see him. They said they were not pleased with his decision and, when Eric insisted he be allowed to do what he wanted, his mother said, "But son, you promised."

Eric knew his mother was right, and he kept the promise he had made. At the college he attended, he received an education that landed him the great job he has today. It was also there he met the wonderful woman to whom he's been married more than twenty years.

Mom, you know best. Your words are worth listening to. Your advice is sound and sure. Your children are wise to follow the direction you give.

Dear God,
thank you for a mom
who knows what I need
to hear and knows how
and when to say it. I am
grateful for what I hear
from you through her.
Amen.

Laughing Moms

The LORD said to Abraham,
"Why did Sarah laugh?"
Genesis 18:13 NRSV

A harried mother was desperately trying to manage her three young children in a supermarket. Neither threats nor bribes had any noticeable effect. The oldest had just knocked down a display of toilet tissue, the youngest was in the shopping cart screaming, and the other one kept running up and down the aisles whooping and hollering. A man standing nearby observed the chaos and asked the mother as she passed by him chasing an errant child, "If you had it to do over again, would you have kids?" "Yes," she shouted back to the man, "but not the same ones."

Mom, you have such a good sense of humor. You can find something funny almost anywhere and in almost anything. Laughter at unlikely times and in improbable places is easy for you. Even when close to tears, you can see the joke in it all.

You use humor so well to take away fear and erase despair. You are always able to look on the light side of a situation and find in it something to laugh about. You know how to not take yourself too seriously. You spot the trivial right away, and never think something is permanent when it is temporary. You understand that a sense of humor is fundamental to both survival and significance.

Your children thank you, Mom, for knowing when to laugh at yourself and for helping them to laugh at themselves when they should. You understand the lifting power of laughter.

Dear God,
thank you for a mom
who knows when and how
to laugh. I am grateful
for her joy that lifts me
up, helps me stand, and
gets me going.
Amen.

A Mom's Affirmations
I Will

1. Know that nothing I do for my chidren is wasted.

2. Believe my children are the world's most valuable natural resource.

3. Believe my children are like Crackerjack boxes; there's a prize in every one of them.

4. Feel that to touch my child is to touch tomorrow.

5. Remember how much Jesus loves the children.

6. Believe my children are innocent when they come from the hand of God.

7. When looking at my children see the face of God.

Things I Need to Do . . .

____1. Gratefully receive every picture my children draw for me.

____2. Stop and look when my children stop to look at a bug in the garden.

____3. Make my children's friends welcome in my house.

____4. Play games with my children that they like.

____5. Keep the cookie jar filled.

____6. Read to my children.

____7. Pray with my children.

A Mother Walks On

The young mother set her foot on the path of life and asked, "Is the way long?" Her guide replied, "Yes, and it is long and hard and you will be old before you reach the end of it, but the end will be better than the beginning."

But the mother was happy in the beginning and did not believe anything could be better. She played with her children and gathered flowers for them along the way. She bathed them in clear streams, and the sun shone on them, and life was good. The young mother said, "Nothing will ever be lovelier than this."

> *Even when I walk through the dark valley of death, I will not be afraid, for you are close beside me. Your rod and your staff protect and comfort me.*
> Psalm 23:4 NLT

Then night came and with it a storm, and the path was dark. The children shook with fear and from cold, and the mother drew them close to her and covered them with a blanket. The children said, "Oh, Mother, we are not afraid, for you are near and hold us close and no harm can come to us." And the mother said, "This is better than the brightness of day, for I have taught my children courage."

And the morning came and there was a hill ahead, and the children climbed and grew weary. The mother also was weary, but she kept saying to her children, "Just a little patience and we will soon be there." So the children climbed, and when they reached the top, they said, "We could not have done it without you, Mother." And the mother, when she lay down to sleep that night, looked up at the stars and said, "This is a better day than the last, for my children have learned fortitude in the face of hardness. Yesterday I gave them courage; today I gave them strength."

And the next day came and with it strange, threatening clouds that darkened the earth. They were clouds of war and hate and evil and revenge. The children groped and stumbled and almost fell, but the mother said, "Look up, children; lift your eyes up to the light." And the children looked up and saw above the clouds an everlasting glory, and it guided them and brought them out of the darkness into the light. And that night the mother said, "This is the best day of all. This is the day I have shown my children God."

The days went on, and the weeks and months and years, and the mother grew old. She became small and bent, but her children were tall and strong. She walked haltingly, but their steps were sure and confident. She was tired, but they were full of energy and determination. When the way was hard, the children helped their mother as she had helped them. When it seemed she couldn't go on, they lifted her up and carried her on. When she forgot something, they remembered it for her. Every time she felt confusion, they gave her clarity. Every time she felt lost, they found her and held her and loved her. When her abilities shrank and her competence decreased, they were able and competent for her.

At last, as mother and children walked on, they came to a hill, and beyond the hill they saw a shining road and golden gates flung wide open. And the mother smiled and said, "Now I have reached the end of my journey, and it is surely true that the end is better than the beginning. It is better because now my children can walk alone, and their children after them." And her children smiled and said, "Oh, Mother, you will always walk with us, even when you have gone through the gates and up the shining road. You will never leave us. We will always know you are with us."

Mom, you are always present to support and affirm your children. You comfort them with a mother's hand, encourage them with a mother's praise, and love them with a mother's heart. Your heart is truly a deep place where they can find true forgiveness. It is a strong place where they can stand until they are able to walk and then run. It is a bright place where they can see through any darkness they experience. Most of all, Mom, it is a believing place where your children can find faith and learn hope and know God.

A Mother's Prayer

Thank you, Lord, for children to hold and love.
They are sweet gifts from above.
When I hear their sounds, I think of you.

Thank you, Lord, for children to lead and guide.
They are my joy and deepest pride.
When I look through their eyes, I see you.

Thank you, Lord, for children to instruct and inspire.
They build within me a glowing fire.
When I am with them, I know you.

Thank you, Lord.
Amen.

Thoughts to Share

Anyone who welcomes a little child like this on my behalf is welcoming me.

Matthew 18:5 NLT

When you take a child by the hand,
you take the mother by the heart.

German Proverb

They will have plenty, and then their children will receive the land.

Psalm 25:13 CEV

In a child's lunch basket are
a mother's thoughts.

Japanese Proverb

God's Spirit joins himself to our spirits to declare that we are God's children.

Romans 8:16 GNT

Depending on Mom

The LORD is my rock, my fortress, and my savior.
Psalm 18:2 NLT

In the musical *Bye Bye Birdie*, Kim McAfee attempts to act grown up by calling her mother by her first name. It's Doris this and Doris that. This, Kim thinks, proves her independence. She is her own person and doesn't need to be running to her mother all the time.

Kim has a crisis in her life, however, and begins feeling insecure. It is then she starts calling Doris *Mother*. It's Mother this and Mother that. Doris responds in motherly ways and does all she can to comfort Kim. Then the crisis gets worse, Kim can't cope, and she starts calling her mother *Mommy*. It's Mommy this and Mommy that. Kim is not nearly so independent as she thought. She needs her mother to get through the tough times.

Mom, so many times your children need you and nobody else will do. No substitute, no surrogate—it has to be you. Only you listen as your children need you to. Only you understand. Only you know what to say. Your children can pour their hearts out to you and receive acceptance, encouragement, and blessing. Mom, your children don't want to see a counselor, confide in a friend, or read a book by an expert. They want you.

You listen closely enough to hear what your children say and look far enough into their lives to see what they need to know about.

Dear God,
thank you for all
the times my mother
reminds me of how
much you love me
and care for me.
Amen.

Glorious Bedtime

I lie down and sleep; I wake again,
for the LORD sustains me.
Psalm 3:5 NRSV

$\mathcal{M}$ickey's mom, eighty-one years old, came to see him
and his family. Driving nearly a thousand miles by herself, she
stayed overnight in a motel, stopped at a shopping outlet, and
came through the door with presents for everyone.

Overwhelmed, Mickey decided it was way past time that he
told his mother how much she meant to him. That evening,
Mickey put his arm around his mom and said, "Mom, do you
know what my earliest memory is?" Mom said she didn't. "I
remember you coming into my room at night and sitting on
the edge of my bed to say my prayers with me." Mickey's mom
chuckled as she recalled those times. "You always brought your
Bible with you. Do you remember that?" Another chuckle.

Mickey went on to tell his mother how he remembered her
reading him stories out of the Bible as her finger moved
smoothly under each word. "Which story did you like best?"
Mom asked.

"Oh, that's easy," Mickey said, "David and Goliath was my all-time favorite."

Mickey's mom then asked if he remembered what she always said at the end of reading that story. "Sure, Mom, you told me that with God by my side I could do anything."

Mom, your children do not forget when you said their prayers with them at night. That was such a wonderful time, and now they know it was a holy time.

Dear God,
thank you for my
mother, who knew you
in her heart and put
you in my heart.
Amen.

Words of Hope & Encouragement

Because of your unfailing love, I
can enter your house; with deepest awe
I will worship at your Temple.

Psalm 5:7 NLT

I trust in your unfailing love;
my heart rejoices in your salvation.

Psalm 13:5 NIV

God's love has been poured into our hearts
through the Holy Spirit that has been given to us.

Romans 5:5 NRSV

Love is patient. Love is kind.
It does not want what belongs to others.

1 Corinthians 13:4 NIrV

[Love] bears all things, believes all things,
hopes all things, endures all things.

1 Corinthians 13:7 NKJV

Thoughts to Share

The heart of a mother is a deep abyss at the bottom of
which you will always find forgiveness.

Honoré de Balzac

No song or story will bear my mother's name.
Yet, so many of the stories I write, that we all write,
are my mother's stories.

Alice Walker

The source of human love is the mother.

African Proverb

I think I'd be a good mother, maybe a little protective.
Like, I would never let the kid out of my body.

Wendy Liebman

I thought my mom's whole purpose was to be my mom.
That's how she made me feel.

Natasha Gregson Wagner

Determined Moms

When Naomi saw that she was determined
to go with her, she said no more to her.
Ruth 1:18 NRSV

No one is more determined than a mom who is committed to the welfare and success of her children. She will leave no stone unturned, no stream uncrossed, no mountain unclimbed to have good things happen for her children. A mom is motivated by the desire to see her children blessed, determined to make good things happen for them, and committed to an unrelenting pursuit of those goals. She believes that success comes in a "can," not in a "can't," and she profoundly resolves to see her children succeed. When she can't find a way for her children, she makes one. She never gives up until the goal is reached and the objective accomplished.

Through all the political and military struggles from the late autumn of 1862 to the early summer of 1863, Abraham Lincoln's resolve, especially concerning the Emancipation

Proclamation, seemed to strengthen rather than weaken. "I may be a slow walker," he remarked, "but I never walk back."

A mother never walks back. She is like the emu and kangaroo that can't move backward. She takes step after step for her children, until the staircase is climbed. Her face is toward a horizon where the sun never sets.

On behalf of your children, Mom, you are a plugger more than willing to pay the price, whatever it is.

Dear God,
thank you for my mom,
who determined I would
have a good life and left
nothing undone so I
could reach that goal.
Amen.

A Mother's Prayers

*For this child I prayed, and the LORD has granted
me my petition which I asked of Him.*
1 Samuel 1:27 NKJV

*O*ne of the strongest images of family life is a mother on her knees asking God to bless her children. Awareness of mothers praying for their children is universal. Everyone can readily see the picture of a mother asking God to be with her children, give them guidance, and protect them. A mother on her knees pouring out her heart on behalf of her offspring is a vivid and well-known portrait of love and caring.

Mothers pray for their children all the time. When expecting a child, a mother gently rubs a hand across her body and asks God to nurture the life within. In the hospital, a mother holds the baby carefully and prayerfully in her arms. Standing over a crib at home, she prays all will be well. When the first word is spoken, the first step taken, a joyful discourse ascends to heaven. That initial day in first grade is bathed in prayer.

Knowing her child is getting ready to start high school, a mother asks God to give good experiences and keep her child from harm. The night before a wedding, the day of a job interview, the time a disappointment takes its toll . . . On and on it goes, mothers on their knees, praying for their children.

Mom, your children appreciate your prayers. They thank you for asking God to guide, direct, and protect them. They feel the power of your prayers in their lives.

Dear God,
thank you for a mother
who talked to you about
me. I am grateful for
each word she said to
you on my behalf.
Amen.

A Mom's Affirmations

I Will . . .

1. Love my children no matter what they do.

2. Do all I can to understand my children.

3. Talk openly with my children about values.

4. Help my children learn from their mistakes.

5. Touch my children often and lovingly.

6. Periodically evaluate my parenting methods.

7. Follow the example of Jesus, who loved the children.

Things I Need to Do . . .

_____1. Have a time each day to celebrate family.

_____2. List three ways to improve my parenting skills and work on them.

_____3. Make sure I know what my children watch on television.

_____4. Be sure I know what kind of neighbors we have.

_____5. Involve my children in church activities.

_____6. Take my children with me to see a sick person.

_____7. Speak positively about people in front of my children.

Training Sessions

Train children in the right way, and
when old, they will not stray.
Proverbs 22:6 NRSV

*M*others train children for decades. Children are bed-
time trained, table trained, potty trained. They are trained to
talk, walk, and relate to other people. Mothers train children to
respond to suggestions, follow directions, and fulfill assign-
ments. Lessons are learned, habits established, and values
developed—all under the direction of mothers. In a child's
early years, a mother is coach, teacher, and trainer.

Some of a mother's training sessions point a child toward
adolescence. Mothers help to instill in their children the strong
sense of confidence they need to prepare for the time when
adolescence invades and deposits its heavy load of self-doubt
and insecurity. Mothers create a safe shelter for the storm of
adolescence. They understand that normal adolescents don't
act normal.

Mom, the training and teaching you did for your children produced results far beyond adolescence. You instilled principles as signposts along life's journey, and created values that became for them watchwords across the years. What you said to them when they were growing up had a lot to do with the way they did grow up. You gave them strength to stand tall in the midst of all circumstances. You gave them courage to do what is right no matter what countering opinions and influences came along.

Mom, your love is always a perfecting love. Everything you do and say is an effort to make your children better people.

Dear God,
thank you for my mom,
who always wanted the
best for me and did
everything she could to
see that I got it.
Amen.

God's Workshop

*You made all the delicate, inner parts of my body
and knit me together in my mother's womb.*
Psalm 139:13 NLT

*Y*ou were God's workshop where your children were made, dear Mom. It was in your womb that God's plan for them took shape. It was there that the groundwork for the many years of their life to come was laid. It was there that happenings of forthcoming decades were set in motion. In your capacity to give birth to them and become their mother was where God's design had its most optimum expression.

For nine months, you and God worked together to bring each child into existence. God drew the blueprint, and you followed it. God created the vessel, and you filled it. You and God loved, cherished, and encouraged your children every minute of the way. You and God thought they were worthy of both divine wisdom and human effort. Your children were counted and confirmed as important and essential parts of the

42

human race. In the Italian language, the literal translation of "to give birth" is "to give to the light." When you gave birth to your children, you gave them the breath and light of life. God spoke his word, you gave yours, and from that holy partnership your children were born.

When you and God made your children, dear Mom, you both had your minds on your work. You did a good job.

Dear God,
thank you for your won-
derful plan of creation
and birth. Thank you
for my mother, who
worked with you to
bring me into the world.
Amen.

A Mother's Prayer

Thank you, Lord, for creating me,

For giving me the light of day,

For wanting me to be,

For guiding me along the way.

Thank you, Lord, for helping me,

In your wisdom and love,

A mother and guide to be,

The greatest gift from above.

Thank you, Lord; thank you so much.

Amen.

Thoughts to Share

We live by faith, not by sight.
2 Corinthians 5:7 NIV

A mother who loves her children imitates
God's love for us, His children.

Christopher de Vinck

*He gives power to the tired and
worn out, and strength to the weak.*
Isaiah 40:29 TLB

To a mother, children are like ideas;
none are as wonderful as her own.

Chinese Saying

*There is a time for everything, and a
season for every activity under heaven.*
Ecclesiastes 3:1 NIV

Ageless Mothers

They will still bear fruit in old age,
they will stay fresh and green.
Psalm 92:14 NIV

Michael and Joyce took his mother shopping for an Easter dress. Every year, they went to a favorite boutique and shopped for something Marie could wear to church on Easter morning. For a long time, Marie's Easter dress had been the talk of church and neighborhood.

This year, Michael and Joyce picked up Marie at the retirement complex where she had lived since her husband died. When they arrived, she was waiting in the lobby, all smiles and full of energy, ready to go shopping. "Let's get going," she said to her son as he stopped to speak to some of the other residents at the center. Michael laughed, put his hand in his mother's, and they left for the boutique.

At the boutique, Marie looked at several dresses, chose one, and took it to the fitting room to try on. Michael winked at Joyce as Marie passed by. Taking a little longer to get the dress on than it used to, she finally emerged from the fitting room and looked around to see Michael and Joyce sitting in chairs waiting for her. She sprightly strutted to them. Her radiance put light all over the room, and her style was a thing to behold. She moved back and forth, smiling at them, and looking absolutely gorgeous. No ninety-one-year-old woman had ever looked so good.

Mom, you are beautiful, so beautiful to your children. The older you get, the more beautiful you are. You are too beautiful for words.

Dear God,
thank you for the
many vivid expressions
of my mom's beauty.
Especially for the
beauty of her heart.
Amen.

Cheerleading Moms

*Therefore encourage one another and build
up each other, as indeed you are doing.*
1 Thessalonians 5:11 NRSV

*M*others run up and down the sidelines of their children's lives, leading cheers. In thought, word, and action they wrap hurrahs around their kids. "You can do it. I know you can," they shout in encouragement for all areas and arenas. The loudest voices at youth baseball games are those of mothers. The crossed fingers and upturned thumbs you see at recitals are attached to the hands of encouraging mothers. The first person to stand when a young man crosses a stage with a diploma in his hand is his mother. The first one up at the end of a play in which a student produced a solid performance is her mother.

Mom, you pick up the megaphone of encouragement and lead cheers on your children's behalf. You understand the importance of encouragement, and you know that a little of it goes a long way. You spark your children's latent potential into

a burning flame of accomplishment with words that support
and buttress them. You put the grip of your faith on their
hearts and speak to them of possibility, perseverance, and
power. You have the ability to break up their discouragement
and lead them to great heights in high places. You truly under-
stand that engines work better when they are oiled. It is
through your supporting sustenance that your children are able
to reach the summit they climb toward.

Mom, you look deeper into your children than anyone
else. You see more there than anyone else can see.

Dear God,
thank you for my mother
and her dreams for me.
Thank you for her
encouragement and
her confidence in me.
Amen.

Words of Hope & Encouragement

*All the people went up after him, and the people were
playing on flutes and rejoicing with great joy, so that
the earth shook at their noise.*

1 Kings 1:40 NASB

*You have filled my heart with greater joy than
when their grain and new wine abound.*

Psalm 4:7 NIV

*With joy you will drink deeply from the
fountain of salvation!*

Isaiah 12:3 NLT

*You have made known to me the ways of life;
you will make me full of gladness with your presence.*

Acts 2:28 NRSV

*You have turned for me my mourning into dancing; You
have loosed my sackcloth and girded me with gladness.*

Psalm 30:11 NASB

Thoughts to Share

A mother's love for her child is like
nothing else in the world.

Agatha Christie

In the sheltered simplicity of the first days after a
baby is born, one sees again the magical closed circle,
the miraculous sense of two people existing
only for each other.

Anne Morrow Lindbergh

A woman who can cope with the terrible
twos can cope with anything.

Judith Clabes

The phrase "working mother" is redundant.

Jane Sellman

Mother is the bank where we deposit
our hurts and worries.

Author Unknown

Moms Tell the Truth

*If you give these instructions to the believers, you will
be a good servant of Christ Jesus, as you feed yourself
spiritually on the words of faith and of the true
teaching which you have followed.*
1 Timothy 4:6 GNT

Joyelle's mom had repeatedly promised her that when
she became eighteen, she could choose whether or not to go to
church. Until then, she had no choice. Joyelle did what her
mom said, but she kept her eye on her eighteenth birthday.
After it came, Joyelle stayed home on Sundays. Mom frequently
asked her if she was going, and the answer was always no.

Some months into her sophomore year in college, Joyelle
decided it was time to prove to her mother that a person did
not have to attend church to be religious. Armed with several
Bible verses, she set out to debate her mother one Saturday
afternoon. The debate heavily favored Joyelle, who couldn't
wait to deliver the final blow. She pointed out to her mother
that there were many hypocrites in the church. Much to
Joyelle's surprise, her mom agreed. As Joyelle began to relax in

her smugness, her mom said there was one thing she knew for sure. "What's that?" her daughter asked haughtily.

"I know that you can stay away from church now and avoid the hypocrites or you can go to heaven and live with them forever."

Joyelle opened her mouth to retort but closed it without a word. She had been bested, because her mother had told the truth.

Mom, your children thank you for sticking to your beliefs and convictions. Thank you for telling them the truth about God.

Dear God,
I believe in you because
my mother told me the
story of your love from
above and the embrace
of your grace.
Amen.

Moms Get There

Blessed are those who show mercy.
They will be shown mercy.
Matthew 5:7 NIrV

Tanya was expecting her first child. He came early, and her parents were across the country attending a business meeting. Tanya's joy abruptly changed to grim reality as a doctor came in the room and reported that her baby had a serious heart defect and probably wouldn't live through the night. The first thing Tanya said upon hearing the news was "I need Mom and I need her right now."

Tanya spent a restless night, tossing, turning, and praying. The next morning, she lay in her bed sobbing in breathless gasps when a knock came at the door. "Come in," she muffled through her crying and tried to pull herself up in a sitting position. The door opened, and Tanya saw the most beautiful sight in the world. Her mother, a bouquet of flowers in her hand and a beaming smile on her face, came through the door and across the room. She laid the flowers on a table, slipped into bed with her Tanya, put her arms around her daughter and told her everything was going to be all right.

From that moment on, Tanya and her mom faced every challenge and problem faithfully, courageously, determinedly, and together.

Mom, you always know when your children need you. You have no confusion about that, and you get to them no matter what it takes.

Dear God,
thank you for
the constancy and
faithfulness of my
mother. When I
need her most,
she always comes.
Amen.

A Mom's Affirmations

I Will . . .

1. Love my children the way God loves me.

2. Not pamper my children too much.

3. Remember my children need presence more than presents.

4. Make my children feel safe.

5. Teach my children about the power of love.

6. Learn when to hold on to my children and when to let go.

7. Keep promises I make to my children.

Things I Need to Do . . .

_____1. Keep a picture book of my children.

_____2. Sit down when my children talk to me.

_____3. See in ordinary events lessons to teach my children.

_____4. Be patient with my children when they are sick.

_____5. Write letters to my children they can keep.

_____6. When wanting to buy my children something because I like it, buy it in my size.

_____7. When my children pull on my clothes, quit washing the dishes.

Mom Takes Over

"God made the world in six days, rested on the seventh day, and my mom took over," quips Latrell as he thinks of what an influence his mother has been on his life for fifty years. A prominent minister in a large city, he attributes his success to his mother's teaching and encouragement.

Latrell's mom married his dad when she was seventeen years old. His brother was born six years later. The marriage of Latrell's parents was tumultuous, but his mom hung on several years until she admitted the marriage was seriously harming the boys. She didn't believe in divorce, but she also didn't believe in standing by while her sons were damaged. She waited one Sunday afternoon while her husband drank himself to sleep. When he was snoring in the upstairs bedroom, she gathered Latrell and his brother, Ervin, quietly removed a screen from the back window, crawled through, and told Latrell to help Ervin out and join them in the backyard. With her finger to her lips in

> *The time came for Mary and Joseph to do what the Law of Moses says a mother is supposed to do after her baby is born. They took Jesus to the temple in Jerusalem and presented him to the Lord.*
> Luke 2:22 CEV

shushing directive, she took Latrell and Ervin up the back alley
and around the corner, where they set out walking for Aunt
Elberta's house on the other side of town. Aunt Elberta and
Uncle Leroy took them in to keep them safe.

That was the day Latrell first became aware of his mother's
incredible strength, a strength that molded him over the years
and helped make him the respected and honored leader he is
today. After she left her husband, Latrell's mom devoted herself
completely to her boys. She worked two jobs to see to it they
had what they needed. She took them to church each Sunday,
attended all their school functions, helped them with their
homework, and exposed them to many opportunities and privi-
leges. Years later, Latrell graduated with a doctor of ministry
degree. A few years after that, Ervin graduated with a doctorate
in anthropology. When Ervin got his degree, someone said,
"Now the Thompson family has a 'pair of docs.'"

Latrell quipped back, "The Thompson family is a paradox."
Latrell's mom agreed that it was certainly against the odds that
she and her sons had been able to accomplish so much.

One of Latrell's fondest memories of his mom's influence
on his life is of when he was home from college for a holiday
after his first semester of classes majoring in business

administration. At the church where he had grown up, a week-long revival meeting was going to take place preceded by a twenty-four-hour prayer vigil. Different church groups signed up to keep vigil at various times during the twenty-four hours.

Having been nurtured in the church and encouraged in prayer by his mother, Latrell signed up with the youth group from eleven o'clock to midnight and with the men's group from midnight to one o'clock. Somewhere in the middle of that time span he felt God speak to him about going into the ministry. It wasn't a new feeling, but it was one he couldn't seem to throw off, as he had in the past.

Latrell struggled with the call until almost three o'clock in the morning when he finally walked the 324 steps back to the house his mother had built so they could be close to everything that went on at the church. Going through the door, he found his mother wide awake and waiting in the front room, wanting to know what in the world was going on. He told her he thought God was calling him to enter the ministry. With the usual economy of words delivered in her direct style, she told him to go back to church and get it settled with the Lord.

Encouraged by his mom's clarity, Latrell returned to the church, where God clearly confirmed his call to the ministry. He went back home about an hour later and peeked through the window to see if his mom had gone to bed. She had not. As Latrell squinted through the glass, he saw his mother in front of her favorite chair, on her knees. She was praying her son through to his decision.

Mothers want their children to find out what God wants and do what God wants. They want their children to know, love, and follow God.

A Mother's Prayer

Before I send my children out to life,

May I teach them how to live.

Before I release them to the world,

May I show them how to give.

Before they move among the people,

May I show them how to forgive.

So that, in living and giving and forgiving,

They may share your grace and spread your love.

Amen.

Thoughts to Share

Anyone who is joined to Christ is a new being;
the old is gone, the new has come.

2 Corinthians 5:17 GNT

The art of mothering is to teach
the art of living to children.

Elaine Heffner

Delight yourself also in the Lord, and He shall give you
the desires of your heart.

Psalm 37:4 NKJV

Blessed be the mothers of the earth.
They combine the practical and the
spiritual into the workable way of human life.

William L. Stinger

Those of steadfast mind you keep in peace—in peace
because they trust in you.

Isaiah 26:3 NRSV

Mothers on a Mission

*When she couldn't hide him any longer she got a little
basket-boat made of papyrus, waterproofed it with tar
and pitch, and placed the child in it. Then she set it
afloat in the reeds at the edge of the Nile.*
Exodus 2:3 MSG

*M*oses was out there on the slopes taking care of his
father-in-law's sheep when God spoke to him from a burning
bush about leading the children of Israel out of Egypt. That
happened because of a mother on a mission. Moses was down
in Egypt transacting God's business with Pharaoh and winning
the release of God's people. He led the children of Egypt
through a tumultuous sea. That happened because of a mother
on a mission. Three months later, Moses led the children of
Israel to the place where he'd seen the burning bush and heard
the speaking God, because of a mother on a mission.

Moses' mother, Jochabed, whose name means "God be
glorified," was that mother on a mission. A mean, old king was
wiping out boy babies, but he wouldn't get hers. She got busy

building a basket. She wove it from leaves she gathered at the river and covered it with tar so water wouldn't seep through. She put a hole in the basket's lid so her baby could breathe and put the basket in the river where he was found and saved.

A mother on a mission builds baskets for her children. She brings them home from the hospital and places them in cribs. She takes her children to her breast and into her heart.

Dear God,
thank you for my
mother, who made
for me a safe and
secure place where
I could learn, grow,
and become who I am.
Amen.

Love That Holds

I have loved you with an everlasting love; therefore
I have continued my faithfulness to you.
Jeremiah 31:3 NRSV

*I*n written Chinese, words are based on pictograms; each word is represented by a picture. The pictogram is designed so that its meaning is apparent at first sight. When the pictogram is seen, there should be no doubt about what the word means. The Chinese character for the word *love*, for instance, is formed by brushstrokes that represent a mother holding a child. A child in a mother's arms is synonymous with the concept and idea of love. You see the mother and think love. *Mother* and *love* are the same.

To be held by a mother is to be loved. It is to be appreciated as a gift from God, affirmed as a miracle of life, acknowledged as a unique individual of promise and possibility. Cradled in a mother's arms, one hears God speak of purpose and plan. In a mother's firm embrace is the gentle whisper of human protection and security, the surround sound of persist-ence and perseverance. When a mother squeezes her child and brushes her face against a rosy cheek, she promises her forever presence. "I will always be here." She smiles her voice of assur-ance. "I will always hold on—I will never let go."

To be in the arms of a mother is to be in the hands of God. It is the sweetest experience this side of heaven.

Dear God,
thank you for the loving
and protecting embrace
of my mom throughout
all my life.
Amen.

Words of Hope & Encouragement

*Whatever is born of God overcomes the world. And this is
the victory that has overcome the world—our faith.*

1 John 5:4 NKJV

*Now faith is being sure of what we hope for
and certain of what we do not see.*

Hebrews 11:1 NIV

*Everything you ask for in prayer will be yours,
if you only have faith.*

Mark 11:24 CEV

*God is able to make all grace abound to you, so that always
having all sufficiency in everything, you may have an
abundance for every good deed.*

2 Corinthians 9:8 NASB

*This same God who takes care of me will
supply all your needs from his glorious riches,
which have been given to us in Christ Jesus.*

Philippians 4:19 NLT

Thoughts to Share

Women, mothers, in your hands more than in those of
anyone else lies the salvation of the world.

Leo Tolstoy

Every time I need a friend, my mom is always there.

Author Unknown

There is no more influential or powerful
role on earth than a mother's.

Charles R. Swindoll

Children are the sum of what mothers
contribute to their lives.

Author Unknown

No matter how perfect your mother thinks you are,
she will always want to fix your hair.

Suzanne Beilenson

Moms Do It All

I can do all things through him who strengthens me.
Philippians 4:13 NRSV

Something that does all the work while you sit there is called automation. It is also called Mother. Put down a soiled shirt, and Mom scoops it up and heads it for the dirty-clothes basket. Fail to put your dinner dishes in the sink, and Mom covers your omission with discerning eye and deft hand. When was the last time you emptied the wastebasket in your room? Or cleaned out your closet?

A teacher showed her preschool students a display of magnets and explained their various uses. It seemed the children understood well, and the teacher was pleased. But just to be sure, she decided to give them a little test. "Who can guess what I am?" she said. "My name starts with an *m* and I pick up things." All the children rang out in united chorus, "Mommy!"

Nobody has a work ethic like a mother. She never lies down on the job and is always up to her ears in work. She seems related to the octopus, arms everywhere doing all kinds of things at the same time. There is not a lazy bone anywhere in a mother's body. A mother's two favorite four-letter words are *hard work*. While others are sleeping, mothers are up and at it. While others are praying for a good harvest, mothers are out in the field hoeing.

A mother understands that what she takes into her hands her children receive into their hearts.

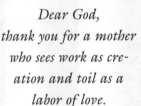

Dear God,
thank you for a mother
who sees work as cre-
ation and toil as a
labor of love.
Amen.

Moms Find Anything

Ask, and you will receive; seek, and you will find;
knock, and the door will be opened to you.
Matthew 7:7 GNT

A mother is the best finder in the world. No military procurement officer can do as well at locating the hidden, retrieving the lost, producing the impossible. A mother has eyes all over her, scanning for the obscure and searching for the abstruse. Her ears can hear the faintest sound that leads to the unseen and the concealed. If eyes and ears aren't enough for the job, a mother's intuition kicks in. A mother's hunch is a fact filed away somewhere just below the conscious level. A mother has feminine radar that hones in on the undetected, the unnoticed, and the unseen. She knows for sure what she doesn't know for certain.

Intuitively or otherwise, a mother can find anything. Her lost-and-found department is always open, and systematically organized. Every item is itemized. Step up to find what eludes your view and escapes your grasp. Come with empty hands and leave with them full of what you've been looking for. A mother can locate what has previously refused to be found. She can find a stray sock in a stuffed drawer, a favorite ring in tall grass, the missing piece of an almost completed puzzle. It has been said that some mothers can find a needle in a haystack.

Mom, when your children can't find the tie that goes with the blue shirt or their school notebook or the car keys, they know whom to ask.

Dear God,
thank you for my mother,
who seeks me when I
have left and finds me
when I am gone.
Amen.

A Mom's Affirmations
I Will ...

1. Understand my children have much to teach me.

2. Be aware my children are watching me.

3. Not keep scorecards on my children.

4. Believe I am a steward of my children.

5. Realize when my children are testing me.

6. Not make my children feel mistakes are sins.

7. Remember that even Mary lost track of Jesus at least one time.

Things I Need to Do . . .

____1. Listen to my children when driving them to activities.

____2. Save money to take my children to a special place.

____3. Keep a deck of cards in the glove compartment of the car.

____4. Make a special family dinner.

____5. Take my children to a library.

____6. Treat each child as an original.

____7. Make a date with the father of my children.

Moms Love Anyway

God proves his love for us in that while we
were still sinners Christ died for us.
Romans 5:8 NRSV

A teenage girl got tired of the restraints of home and
ran away. She wanted to be free, to do things her own way. For
a while it worked. Then she fell on hard times, lost her job,
and ended up living in a rescue mission in a city teeming with
confusion and evil. Three years went by, and the girl's mother
did not hear a word from her daughter. Then one day, the
rumor mill hinted at her whereabouts. The mother heard that
her daughter was in an unidentified rescue mission in a large
city nearly four hundred miles away. Her mother went immedi-
ately to that city and visited more than thirty rescue missions.
She did not see her daughter in any of them, but in each she
left a picture of herself, beneath which she had written, "Come
home. I love you!"

One day, having worn out her welcome at several rescue stations, the girl wandered into a different one for a free meal. While eating hungrily what was put before her, she glanced around the room and on a bulletin board saw the picture of her smiling mother saying to her, "Come home. I love you." Two days later, a tired and weary daughter made her way home and fell into the wide-open arms of her mother.

Thank you, Mom, for keeping the door to your heart unlocked at all times. Your children always know they can go home to you.

Dear God,
thank you for my mom,
who always stands at the
door, watches for my
return, and runs out to
meet me when I do.
Amen.

The Worth of a Mother

*Look at the birds of the air, for they neither sow nor
reap nor gather into barns; yet your heavenly Father
feeds them. Are you not of more value than they?*
Matthew 6:26 NKJV

A financial analyst studied the monetary value of duties
performed by mothers in their homes. He assigned a dollar
amount to the jobs of nursemaid, cook, housekeeper, chauffeur,
nurse, dietician, and other services provided. It was calculated
that the labor performed by the average mother would cost the
family more than forty thousand dollars a year. This figure did
not include teacher, coach, interior decorator, religious educa-
tion instructor, and other titles of a mother. It would cost many
millions of dollars each year to have someone else do what
mothers do. The amount is astounding. The contribution
mothers make is priceless, their value inestimable, their worth
incomparable.

While it's true that money is a lousy way of keeping score,
one cannot discount the value and worth of what mothers do

for their children. Holding them steady for their first inde-
pendent steps, teaching them to tie their shoes, walking them
down the block to their initial day of school, reading them
wonderful and warm stories at night and then remaining on
the edge of their beds to say prayers with them, and walking
with them each step of the way through all the years could
never be measured in dollars and cents.

There is no way, Mom, that your children can put a price
tag on what you do for them. And, while they do not know
the price, they are aware of the value.

Dear God,
thank you for my mom,
who gives so much so
I can be who I am
and do what I do.
Amen.

A Mother's Prayer

Thank you, God, for those you give to me.

Let the little children come.

The gift of yourself through them is amazing.

Let the little children come.

I see in a child's face your grace, your love from above.

Let the little children come.

Your beauty they show; your touch I know.

Let the little children come.

*Thank you, God, for the little
children who come to me.*

Amen.

Thoughts to Share

Heaven and earth will disappear,
but my words will remain forever.

Mark 13:31 NLT

A mother is not a person to lean on but
a person to make leaning unnecessary.

Dorothy Canfield Fisher

God cares for you, so turn all
your worries over to him.

1 Peter 5:7 CEV

We are transfused into our children and feel more
keenly for them than for ourselves.

Marie de Sévigné

The Lord is my light and my salvation;
whom shall I fear? The Lord is the defense
of my life; whom shall I dread?

Psalm 27:1 NASB

Moms Make You Feel Good

Peter: you are a rock, and on this rock foundation
I will build my church, and not even death will
ever be able to overcome it.
Matthew 16:18 GNT

$\mathcal{M}$om, you put the wind in your children's sails and help them go farther than they thought possible. As Jesus did that day when he affirmed Peter's worth, you know how to focus on your children's value and potential. They can start every day knowing you believe in them and have faith they can do that day what they have to do. You spread hope, confidence, and assurance all over them with your estimation of who they are and yet can be. You find glorious possibilities in everything they do. You acclaim even their thoughts and ideas, readily endorse their plans and dreams. Regarding your children, you seem to have unlimited optimism.

You always manage to see something good or helpful in what they do. Each day they try to be special to those they meet because you think they are. Sometimes when they are tempted to say no to themselves about something, they hear your great and triumphant yes ringing in their heart. You are like Jesus, who called Nathanael "a true Israelite, in whom there is nothing false" and said of John the Baptist that "there was none greater born to women." Mom, your confidence in your children makes their day, and sends them on their way with a song in their hearts and a gleam in their eyes.

Mom, you make your children feel important, capable, and valuable. Your affirmation puts them on their feet and keeps them there.

Dear God,
thank you for the
encouragement and
affirmation you send
through my mother, who
loves me and believes I
am special.
Amen.

Moms Stay at It

I press on toward the goal to win the prize for which
God has called me heavenward in Christ Jesus.
Philippians 3:14 NIV

*M*om, you give new meaning to the word *tenacity.* You
have more stick-to-it-tive-ness than most people. When others
come to the end of their ropes, you tie a knot in yours and
hang on. You take a licking and come up ticking. You keep on
keeping on. The Portuguese language has a word that suits
you, Mom. It defines someone who has the ability to hang in
there no matter what. The word is *garra*, and it means
"claws." Someone who has that quality burrows into the side
of a cliff and hangs on. Mom, you've done that many times.
You've kept going long after even you yourself thought you
couldn't.

Mom, you've run into many walls over the years. There
were times when money was short and you somehow found a
way to make the budget come out all right. You had some

rough sledding sometimes with family relationships, but you came up with a plan to bring about reconciliation and establish peace. There were sicknesses and job disappointments, too, but you confidently moved from plan A to plan B. When you ran into a wall, Mom, you figured out how to climb it or work your way around it or go through it.

Mom, you can do anything because you know how to stick to it long enough. You don't fold up, Mom; you hold up.

Dear God,
thank you for my mom,
who teaches me to con-
quer by continuing. I'm
glad that she stays by my
side at all times.
Amen.

Words of Hope & Encouragement

*The LORD is good; he protects his people in times of trouble;
he takes care of those who turn to him.*

Nahum 1:7 GNT

*I lift up my eyes to the hills—from where will
my help come? My help comes from the LORD,
who made heaven and earth.*

Psalm 121:1–2 NRSV

*Let us come boldly to the throne of our gracious God.
There we will receive his mercy, and we will find
grace to help us when we need it.*

Hebrews 4:16 NLT

*Heal me, O LORD, and I shall be healed; save me,
and I shall be saved, for You are my praise.*

Jeremiah 17:14 NKJV

*The One who has chosen you is faithful.
He will do all these things.*

1 Thessalonians 5:24 NIrV

Thoughts to Share

Anyone who thinks mother love is as soft and
golden-eyed as a purring cat should see a cat
defending her kittens.

Pam Brown

To love our children is to see them, respect them,
share life with them . . . and always let them go.

Anne Wilson Schaef

One mother achieves more than a hundred teachers.

Jewish Proverb

The cheerful voice, the happy laughter of a mother,
make home a lovely place to be.

Elizabeth Beck

My mother made a brilliant impression upon
my childhood life. She shone for me like the
evening star. I loved her dearly.

Winston Churchill

Moms Are Responsible

I heard the voice of the Lord, saying,
"Whom shall I send, and who will go for Us?"
Then I said, "Here am I. Send me!"
Isaiah 6:8 NASB

$\mathcal{M}$om, you are the one who taught your children to be responsible. When they were small, you insisted they pick up their toys and put them away. You instructed them to clear the table of their dishes and put them in the sink. You are the one who taught your children how to wash out the bathtub, and your children can probably still make a bed with the best of them.

You taught your children to be responsible for what they do, no matter how they feel about it. "Do it anyway!" you said. You never let your children expect someone else to do for them what they were supposed to do for themselves. You never let your children use excuses for inaction. You taught your children that *rationalization* is just a fancy word for lying to yourself. You also taught them that privilege and responsibility are

the two sides of the same coin. You reminded your children on
several occasions that it is a privilege to have something to be
responsible for. When your children complained about some-
thing in their world, you told them that they were responsible
for making it better. You said that they have ability and are
responsible for using it.

Mom, you teach your children to be honest, trustworthy,
dependable, and responsible. There are no better lessons.

Dear God,
thank you for the
many ways in which
my mother instructed
my faithfulness and
made me responsible
for what I have and
who I am.
Amen.

Moms Know What to Say

*Thus says the LORD: Go down to the house of
the king of Judah, and speak there this word.*
Jeremiah 22:1 NRSV

A mother knows what to say and when to say it. Her
words are contextually relevant and chronologically appropri-
ate. Not too early, not too late, right on time. Not too much,
not too little, just the right amount. Neither complex nor sim-
plistic, a mother's words get to the point. Her words, while
not consistently heeded, are always heard. Nobody has to tell a
mother to speak up. If there's a communication gap in her
house, she's not responsible for it.

A visitor from another country said he noticed that people
in this country, after making some remark, say, "In other
words," and then go on to say it another way. No mother
needs other words to say what she intends to say. She says it
clearly the first time. When a mother speaks to her child, it is
clear that child is loved and cared about. The words a mother

speaks are words that will assist and help. She uses them to get through to her child. She wants to reach the person to whom she is speaking. She wants her words to make a difference in the lives of her children.

A mother's words are servant words. She sends them forth on behalf of her children to instruct, inspire, and enable.

Dear God,
thank you for the frank
and forthright words of
my mother, through
which you communicate
your purpose and
plan for me.
Amen.

A Mom's Affirmations

I Will . . .

1. Lift my children up, never put them down.

2. Find something each day to brag on my children about.

3. Make my children proud of me.

4. Be sure my children know I love God.

5. Praise God in front of my children.

6. Use clean language in front of my children.

7. Keep habits I want my children to have.

Things I Need To Do...

_____1. Give my children chores to do.

_____2. Help them with chores, when necessary.

_____3. Encourage my children to keep a diary or journal.

_____4. Take my children and their friends to a movie.

_____5. Volunteer the entire family for a church project.

_____6. Teach Bible verses to my children.

_____7. Take my children to a charity where they can help.

A Longtime Mom

Arletta had never had so much fun planning a birthday party. Neither had Reginald, Tamika, or Darnell. Since Arletta was geographically closest to the birthday girl, she did most of the hands-on planning and nearly all the legwork, but she and her three siblings consulted one another frequently by cell phone, e-mail, and fax. Thoughts and ideas were shared on the phone, long-forgotten pictures were faxed to those who shrieked delight at their arrival, and a constant barrage of e-mail messages about things suddenly remembered went back and forth between Georgia, Vermont, Michigan, and Arizona. This had been going on for nearly five months in preparation for the big September day.

Once I was young, and now I am old. Yet I have never seen the godly forsaken.
Psalm 37:25 NLT

When the day came, there would be a sit-down dinner at a hotel in the city where the birthday honoree lived. Almost two hundred people were expected, including reporters from all the area newspapers. One television station had promised an appearance. A special assistant to the mayor, representing the city in which the celebrant had lived all her life, would make a

short speech. The honoree's current pastor would say some-
thing in her honor. Hopefully, at least nine former pastors
would be able to attend and, if they chose, would also speak.
An agency for runaway children, the hospital's volunteer service
department, and a clothes-closet ministry would send represen-
tatives—all groups to which the honoree had given her time
and talent. The evening's entertainment would include a gospel
choir from the honoree's church and a jazz band in which both
her sons had played when they were growing up. It would be a
grand celebration, for sure.

Arletta had just put the finishing touches on a final draft of
the evening's program. Reginald had provided a drawing for
the front cover of the program; Tamika had written a special
prayer; and Darnell had a high-school friend in the printing
business who would produce enough copies for everybody who
came and some to save for posterity.

Arletta looked at her list of things yet to be accomplished
and clicked them off in her mind one by one: flowers to order,
transportation for some of the honoree's older friends, last-
minute menu check with the caterer, and two or three other
items. Tamika planned to arrive from Arizona two days before
the celebration and could help her with last-minute details and

any suddenly discovered omissions. Reginald was flying in from Michigan one day before the momentous event, and Darnell had a night-owl flight from Vermont the eve of the big bash.

September 17 arrived, and Sally Mae Turner awoke in the assisted-living complex that was operated by her church. At breakfast in the dining room with fellow residents, she was congratulated all the way around. A few people gave her cards, but most kept their remembrances for the evening party. At a downtown café, where they'd hung out as kids, Arletta, Reginald, Darnell, and Tamika chatted around eggs and grits about the limousine they'd rented in which to pick up their mama and the special bouquet of flowers that Sally Mae would carry in her arms when she entered the hotel. The four siblings spent most of breakfast time talking about what would be, for them, the highlight of the evening.

The last item on the agenda was a testimony from each of Sally Mae's four children about her love for them and her passion for their lives. Arletta, the oldest at seventy-seven, would be first to speak. She would be followed, in turn, by her three siblings. With great sentiment and deep emotion, Sally Mae's offspring discussed what they would say on the occasion of their mother's one-hundredth birthday.

Mom, the years you have lived are like a bank account into which you make deposits and your children make withdrawals. You deposit hard work, and your children withdraw station and security. You exhibit deep trust in God, and your children acquire a life of faith and prayer. You invest solid values and high principles, and your children earn a moral foundation on which to stand and live their lives admirably and successfully. You model good ways to get along with people, and your children understand the challenges and rewards of human relationships. You teach lessons of courage in the face of daily life, and your children learn how to depend on God for every step they take.

Your children have reaped, dear Mom, because you have sown.

A Mother's Prayer

For the curiosity of my children,
For all the questions they ask,
For each and every thing they want to know,
I give you thanks, O Lord.

For sicknesses that didn't last,
For wounds that eventually healed,
For disappointments that became distant,
I give you thanks, O Lord.

For moments of prayer at bedtime,
For words of gratitude around the table,
For all times together with you and my children,
I give you thanks, O Lord.

Thoughts to Share

*Since we have been made right in God's sight
by faith, we have peace with God because of what Jesus
Christ our Lord has done for us.*

Romans 5:1 NLT

No language can express the power and
beauty and heroism of a mother's love.

Edwin H. Chapin

*I am the vine, you are the branches. Those who abide in
me and I in them bear much fruit.*

John 15:5 NRSV

The walks and talks we have with our two-year-olds
in red boots have a great deal to do with the values
they will cherish as adults.

Edith F. Hunter

*We know that God is always at work for
the good of everyone who loves him.*

Romans 8:28 CEV

Moms Listen

*While he was still speaking, a bright cloud
enveloped them, and a voice from the cloud said,
"This is my Son, whom I love; with him I am
well pleased. Listen to him!"*
Matthew 17:5 NIV

Mom, nobody listens to your children the way you do.
You listen with so much love that your children know for sure
you understand everything they say. You keep your eyes fixed
on them; your eyes never stray from attending to your chil-
dren's every word. You don't interrupt with judgment but let
them finish before giving assessment and opinion. You never
superimpose your story on their stories, or make them feel that
what they are saying isn't important. You honor their emotions
and sensitivities, and you never tell them they shouldn't feel
the way they do. You affirm, even flatter them with the way
you listen. You listen with outstretched ears, loving eyes, and
encouraging heart.

You understand that God gave you two ears and only one

tongue so you could listen more than you speak. If you need to persuade your children about something, you do it by listening to their words much more than by speaking yours. You listen without assumption, Mom, and project no pretense. The just and fair way in which you listen is why your children are able to talk to you the way they do. It is why they can tell you how they really feel about something. It is why they can always tell you the truth. More than anything, the way you listen always gives God a chance to speak to them.

Mom, you know that your children need a good listening-to. You understand that the beginning of wisdom is hearing what is really said.

Dear God,
thank you for the
listening ears, eyes, and
heart of my dear and
loving mother.
Amen.

Moms Have Faith

I assure you, even if you had faith as small as a
mustard seed you could say to this mountain,
"Move from here to there," and it would
move. Nothing would be impossible.
Matthew 17:20 NLT

Mothers have more faith than anybody. Maybe it's because they work so closely with God in getting their babies born. Being a part of the creation team, they work hand in hand, heart to heart, with God's divine design for life and love. Mothers talk to God and listen to what God says back. They consult God about large issues, confer with God about minutiae, and check daily agenda items out with God. Mothers want to know what God thinks, what God wants. The first number entered in the directory of every mom's cell phone is heaven.

Perhaps it is not so much that mothers possess faith as it is that faith possesses them. Possesses them so much they don't have to see an entire road to walk in front of them. In faith, the first step is enough. Mothers believe that having God on their side puts them in a majority position. They believe God is faithful and their faith is a response to God's faithfulness. That is why they can confidently shove off from the shore even when they don't have the gear necessary to get to the other side. All they have to do, moms know, is lift their sails and God will send the wind.

Mothers have faith to make decisions before they've solved all the problems.

Dear God,
thank you that I
have the example of
my mother's faith to
follow in my life.
Amen.

Words of Hope & Encouragement

Those who wait for the LORD will gain new strength;
they will mount up with wings like eagles.

Isaiah 40:31 NASB

Be still before the LORD, and wait patiently for him.

Psalm 37:7 NRSV

I waited patiently for the LORD;
he turned to me and heard my cry.

Psalm 40:1 NIV

Make sure that your endurance carries you all
the way without failing, so that you may be
perfect and complete, lacking nothing.

James 1:4 GNT

It is good that one should wait quietly
for the salvation of the LORD.

Lamentations 3:26 NRSV

Thoughts to Share

My mother was the making of me.

Thomas Edison

Children will not remember you for the
material things you have provided, but for
the feeling that you cherished them.

Richard L. Evans

The mother's heart is the child's schoolroom.

Henry Ward Beecher

Making the decision to have a child is momentous.
It is to decide forever to have your heart go walking
around outside your body.

Elizabeth Stone

There is nothing sweeter than
the heart of a pious mother.

Martin Luther

Moms Forgive

*You have forgiven your people's sins
and pardoned all their wrongs.*
Psalm 85:2 GNT

In 1983, Pope John Paul went to a prison to see Mehmet Ali Agca, the young man who had tried to assassinate him. In a bare, white-walled cell the pope tenderly held the hand that had held the gun Agca had used to try to kill him. For twenty-one minutes, the report said, he sat with his would-be assassin. Nobody but the two of them and God know what was said, but it is certain the pope spoke words of forgiveness to the young man.

Mothers hold the hands of their children of all ages and speak to them authentic words of forgiveness. They do not indelibly write down every wrong with the pencil of a long memory; rather, they take out the eraser of forgiveness and rub it firmly across the deeds and words of their children. Mothers put their loving arms of clemency around the hearts of their children and walk with them as if nothing much had happened. Mothers bury the hatchet and never leave the handle sticking out of the ground. They don't even mark the spot. A mother has her finger on the Delete key at all times. Mothers love their children by forgiving them and opening the door of the future to them.

Nothing in the world bears the impress of God so surely as a mother's forgiving love.

Dear God,
I am grateful for
the forgiving love
and the loving
forgiveness of my
wonderful and
gracious mother.
Amen.

Moms Forget

Forget each wrong I did when I was young.
Show how truly kind you are and remember me.
Psalm 25:7 CEV

A young man borrowed the family car without permission. He thought he could have it home and back in the garage before his mother missed it, since she was out for the evening. He hadn't reckoned on getting rear-ended at the first intersection he came to. There was no way to conceal the damage, so he took the car home and parked it in the garage. He closed the garage door, went into the house, and spent the evening agonizing over how to tell his mom what had happened.

The next day he told her everything, and added a long and sincere apology. His mother walked with him to the garage and looked long, hard, and silently at the damaged car. Then she said, "Our insurance will cover it. It wouldn't have covered the broken trust between us if you'd tried to cover up what happened. Your apology took care of everything." A week later the son, still guilt-ridden, came to his mother and said, "Mom, in case they raise our insurance because of the accident, I am willing to earn money to pay the difference in the premium." Mom looked up from the newspaper she was reading at the breakfast table and said, "What accident?"

Mothers have wonderfully short memories. They remember to forget. The scent of past misdeeds does not catch up with them.

Dear God,
thank you for all the
times my mom forgot
something I said, did,
or threatened to do.
Amen.

A Mom's Affirmations

I Will ...

1. Believe the best about my children.

2. Keep secrets my children ask me to.

3. Celebrate what my children are becoming.

4. Ask my children their opinions.

5. Speak to my children about their faith in God.

6. Be a forgiving mother.

7. Be an available mother.

Things I Need to Do . . .

_____1. Keep my children's favorite snacks on hand.

_____2. Plan a daily prayer time for my family.

_____3. Get my children talking about what they are thankful for.

_____4. Take children with me to visit neighbors.

_____5. Get creative toys for my children that challenge them.

_____6. Have little gifts in my purse for my children.

_____7. Keep a camera in the car for candid pictures.

No-Matter-What Moms

When they pray, God will answer; they will worship
God with joy; God will set things right for them again.
Job 33:26 GNT

Mothers are no-matter-what people. They accept their children no matter what they do. To them, their children will never be unfit. Their love wraps itself around their children. Their children are never too ornery or naughty to remain outside the embrace of their mother's love.

No-matter-what mothers point to the truth about no-matter-what God. God accepts people just as they are and, sometimes, in spite of what they are. No one can wander away from God far enough to exceed the reach of God's grace, mercy, and love. God seeks people out and brings people back. God waits for his people's return and welcomes them home. God heals wounds and then ignores the scars. God loves his children just as they are, and not as God hopes they will become. Of course, God doesn't want his children to stay as they are, but change is not a prerequisite for God's acceptance. Everyone can sing the great hymn "Just As I Am" with true and personal meaning. No one has to get qualified or certified for God to open the door of grace. Win or lose, God covers his kids.

God is like a mother, putting the arms of love tightly and securely around his children at all times.

Dear God,
thank you for loving me
nevertheless and no
matter what. Thank
you for my mother,
who does the same.
Amen.

Moms Know Their Kids

I am the good shepherd. I know my sheep,
and my sheep know me.
John 10:14 NIrV

The first day of kindergarten, a five-year-old boy was nervous and upset. The teacher tried to calm him down, but nothing worked. Finally, she agreed to place a call to his mother and let him talk to her. The teacher dialed the number, waited for it to ring, and handed the phone to the little guy. But when his mother said hello, he was too nervous and upset to speak. He didn't say a word, or make a sound. So the mother said, "Who is this?"

The boy burst into tears and said, "Mom, did you forget me already?"

Mothers know who their children are. They understand the full identity of their offspring well and intimately. They know both the source and meaning of quirks, preferences, and moods. They know the dreams and dares of their children, as well as the insecurities and uncertainties. Mothers have a sensitivity that cuts through symptoms to sources and gets down to the bottom line where their children live and function. Mothers peel off labels put on their children by others or by the children themselves. They are able to put their hands instantly on every spot in the souls of their children.

Mothers read between the lines, hear between the sounds, and feel deep down into the hearts of their children.

Dear God,
thank you for a
mother who knows at
all times who I am
and who I am not.
Amen.

A Mother's Prayer

I thank you, God, for all the firsts.
First sign of a heartbeat,
First time in my arms,
First night in the crib.

I thank you, God, for all the beginnings:
Beginning of a mother's love,
Beginning of a mother's prayers,
Beginning of a mother's hopes.

I thank you, God, for all the starts:
The start of trust and dependence,
The start of joy and laughter,
The start of knowing you are always with me.
Amen.

Thoughts to Share

Since we are his children, we will share his treasures—for everything God gives to his Son, Christ, is ours, too.

Romans 8:17 NLT

You can never really live anyone else's life, not even your child's. The influence you exert is through your own life, and what you've become yourself.

Eleanor Roosevelt

God has given us his Spirit. That's why we don't think the same way that the people of this world think. That's also why we can recognize the blessings that God has given us.

1 Corinthians 2:12 CEV

The mother is and must be, whether she knows it or not, the greatest, strongest, and most lasting teacher her children have.

Hannah Whitall Smith

My grace is sufficient for you, for My strength is made perfect in weakness.

2 Corinthians 12:9 NKJV

Taught to Ask

*Only ask, and I will give you the nations as your
inheritance, the ends of the earth as your possession.*
Psalm 2:8 NLT

When Zachary was a boy, his mother made him ask
people for things. When they ate at a restaurant and needed
ketchup for his fries, his mother insisted he ask the server to
get it for them. At the library, when they couldn't find a book,
Zachary's mother sent him to the desk to ask the librarian
where the book could be found. By teaching her son to ask for
things, Zachary's mother followed closely the teaching of
Jesus, who said that if believers want to receive, they should
ask.

During the Spanish-American War, Colonel Teddy
Roosevelt commanded a regiment of roughriders in Cuba. He
became deeply attached to his men and became greatly con-
cerned when any of them became ill. Roosevelt heard that
Clara Barton, who organized the Red Cross, had received a

supply of food for the soldiers under her care. He bid her to sell a portion of it to him for the sick men of his regiment. His bid was refused, which troubled him greatly, especially since he had offered to pay for the food out of his own pocket. He went to Clara Barton and said to her, "I must have food for my sick soldiers. How do I get it?"

She replied, "Just ask for it, Colonel."

Moms know the correlation between asking and receiving, and teach it to their children.

Dear God,
thank you that my
mother taught me to ask
for what I need. When I
ask, I always gain.
Amen.

Moms Know Attitude

I am absolutely sure that not even death or life
can separate us from God's love. Not even angels
or demons, the present or the future, or any
powers can do that.
Romans 8:38 NIrV

Moms teach their children that life can get better if they change their attitude. Moms know a good attitude is more important to their children than education, money, or anything else. A positive attitude is a rope hanging all the way down the mountain children must climb to get to where they want to be. When attitude is right, progress is inevitable. With a constructive outlook, there is no barrier too high and no valley too deep. No dream is too large for those who think positively. No challenge is too formidable.

Moms teach their children that while they cannot always control what goes on outside them, they can always control what goes on inside them. From the time a child throws that first temper tantrum, moms tell them they are only an attitude away from a different and far healthier response. Mothers know that accomplishment and achievement begin at the point of attitude. Mothers say to their children that the more often they have a good attitude, the more often they have a good day. Mothers know that with a good attitude, the battle is won before it is begun.

Going through a school gym one day, a mother saw a motto on a wall that she wrote down, took home, and taught to each of her children. "Talent wins games. Attitude wins gold medals."

Dear God,
thank you for my
mother, who teaches me
the best thing about any
task is the spirit in
which it is done.
Amen.

Words of Hope & Encouragement

In God I trust; I am not afraid.
What can a mere mortal do to me?

Psalm 56:11 NRSV

Let us be bold, then, and say, "The Lord is my helper,
I will not be afraid. What can anyone do to me?"

Hebrews 13:6 GNT

Be strong and take heart, all you who hope in the LORD.

Psalm 31:24 NIV

Give your burdens to the LORD, and he will take care
of you. He will not permit the godly to slip and fall.

Psalm 55:22 NLT

The eternal God is a dwelling place,
and underneath are the everlasting arms.

Deuteronomy 33:27 NASB

Thoughts to Share

To describe my mother would be to write
about a hurricane in its perfect power.

Maya Angelou

Mother is the name for God in the lips
and hearts of little children.

William Makepeace Thackery

A positive mom doesn't take away her children's
troubles; she teaches them how to look for the
hand of God in the midst of them.

Karol Ladd

My mother's menu consisted of two choices:
Take it or leave it.

Buddy Hackett

No woman can be strong, gentle, pure, and good
without the world being better for it, without
somebody being helped and comforted by the
very existence of that goodness.

Phillips Brooks

Moms Can Party

"Bring the fatted calf here and kill it,
and let us eat and be merry; for this my son
was dead and is alive again; he was lost
and is found." And they began to be merry.
Luke 15:23–24 NKJV

Moms know how to celebrate the lives of their children. Each birthday, there is a party with presents, ice cream, and friends. Sometimes, moms reserve a whole section of a fun place for the celebration. Mothers sometimes hire clowns who come to a party and make wonderful animals out of balloons. And it's not just birthdays that mothers know how to celebrate. Every accomplishment and achievement of their children is a time of rejoicing. When children learn to tie shoes, moms jump up and down like the kids have gone to the moon. Or, before that, how about the first step a child takes? Mothers follow a child through life, and the occasions for celebration never cease, no matter how old the children are. Mothers know how to celebrate the lives of their children.

That puts moms in close step with Jesus Christ, for he is the one who talked about the terrific parties thrown after finding a lost sheep, a lost coin, and a lost son. He is the one who likened the kingdom of God to a banquet, a feast, a party. Jesus talked incessantly about sharing the joy of life with other people in great bursts of festivity and merriment.

Moms can throw parties for their children. They know where the hats and horns are, and how to get them out.

Dear God,
thank you for my mom,
who knows how to have
fun and makes every
celebration a time of joy.
Amen.

Moms Get Tough

*Be brave and fight hard to protect our people
and the towns of our LORD God.*
1 Chronicles 19:13 CEV

People who lived in Ivan's hometown knew better than to be unfair to him in any way. If they did anything to him that was uncalled for, they would have to answer to his mother. You didn't mess with Harriett's boy—not if Harriett knew about it, and it seemed she always did. Nothing much that happened to Ivan escaped Harriett. When she found out someone had been unfair to her son, she was out of the house and down the street to defend her boy.

Mothers have courage to stick up for their children. When it comes to defending their own, they are not reticent or reluctant. If mothers are naturally shy or bashful, they overcome such characteristics when their children are wronged. The mildest mannered mom becomes a tornado when she perceives some offense has been done to her children. Most animals will fight to the death to protect their young, and nothing motivates a mother like her children being threatened in some way. On behalf of their children, mothers wear the badge of courage.

When it comes to their kids, mothers flex the muscles of courage developed by pumping the iron of commitment, loyalty, and devotion.

Dear God,
thank you for my mom,
who is not afraid to
speak up and stand up
for her children.
Amen.